SHATTERED GLASS

*A Collection of poetry about
Broken pieces of me*

N.AKIN

This book is dedicated to my baby girl. I would also like to dedicate this work to anyone suffering from a broken heart. Loving the wrong person is not easy. You will find solace as long as you do not allow whom someone else is to change the nature of who you are.

SBN: 9781718020689

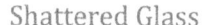

To the butterfly kisses, I could never get enough of. Mommy loves you very much baby girl.

Contents of this book:

Truth Hurts

Dedicated to "The Surgeon"

The truth is ugly

Often unclothed

Indifferent

Unattractive

Not willing to leave your heart unharmed

Cloaked in unnecessary ruthless words

Often better left unheard.

-Truth

I am creative

Because I was created

By a creator

Who is creative

Since I was created in its image

I can create.

These thighs despise lies

If you want to get in between them

The truth can wedge your way in.

Sent:

He (you) surgically removed my heart

Placed it back

Expecting it to function the same

Read:

Response:

"I'm sorry"

-Going forward we will refer to him as

"The Surgeon"

Unsaid:
I don't' want to be something to do

When you've got nothing to do

Someone to talk to

When you have no one to talk to

I want to be the one you think about

Can't bear to do without

The one you talk about

Be the one who

You can't wait to get next to

The one you make love to

The one and only

Not only

When actuality

Is not reality.

-Note to the surgeon

Unsaid:

If you're seeing her

I'll bring a blindfold

Just want you to see *me*

With your eyes closed.

-Note to the surgeon

Unsaid:

Questions:

Why do we stop speaking?

Only to speak again

Why do we start leaving?

Only to come back as if we never left

Longing for caress

Why do you fail to show emotion?

Then respond to every question

As if we're on the same page?

And set the stage

Responses never delayed

I am the reason

Never a new season

I am keeping this up

I follow up

Only to be told turn around

With the monotone sound.

Go back home

Here isn't where you belong

Your voice

Your choice

Undemonstratively

Carefree

Emotionless

Nevertheless

I'll take the hint as you suggest.

-Note to the surgeon

Unsaid:

Would you believe me

If I told you

That I enjoyed every minute of it?

Falling that is

Right down to the last second.

-Note to the surgeon

Felt as though I lost someone close to me

In a sense, I guess I did

To the depths of despair

I seemed to be heading

How could you not attempt to save me?

-Note to the surgeon

Unsaid:

I poured out my heart that day

Fear deep within me

Expecting the reaction I've received

Multiple times before

But I never learned

Not to trust you

With my most prized possession

I handed you my heart

And you handed it back

Stated it never belonged to you

And you did not want the gift of my love

You could not accept it

Because it is not what you wanted.

-Note to the surgeon

Pick up the pieces baby girl:

Do not dwell here long

This painful place he has brought you to

The place GPS could not find

Get back in your vehicle

Drive back to where you were

Start your journey all over again.

-Note to self

Unsaid:

I send love notes

Then I delete them

Before you get a chance to read

Then you ask'

"What was in the deleted message?"

And I say *"nothing"*

"It was something meant for someone else"

At times that is the truth

Many times I find it difficult, to be honest with

even myself that I could be so carelessly crazy

about someone.

So I told the truth:

For it will me set me free they said,

And it did!!

Felt free for that moment "Free"

"Free from loving you

Free from the burden of keeping that love a

secret from you

I couldn't breathe when I sent the message

Had a brief moment of panic as I hit send.

Unsaid:
Perplexed by the entire situation

Misinterpreted words unmentioned

Not sure how to handle the misread signs

Read between too many lines

That you so boldly lay before me

Only to remind me that **we**

Are **not** an item

No matter how many times I come

You come, and we come

Always welcomed

To your door, my refuge for sure

Not now, or then, and when

I think we are getting to an understanding

A misunderstanding

Is what you present to me

Explaining again, again, and again, **loudly**

Until I can see

That me, you, WE cannot be what I perceived

us to be.

-Note to the surgeon

I walk around like a broken soul

Broken spirit still seeking expression

I am forever weeping over someone or

something.

Clinging to the allusion of a past

That I could never bring back

I need healing my heart needs healing

My soul is crying out to me for help!

To help her out of this saddened state

I am trying I am lying to myself

When I say I don't need help.

-Soul seeking

Unsaid:

I wish I were not so forgiving at times

If you come to me right now

I will wholeheartedly take you back

As your words flashed across my screen

They were forgiven as I read them.

-Note to the surgeon

Unsaid:

I always forgave you

Even when you were not sorry

And will always forgive you

Even when you are NOT sorry

For things you were not aware you did

And are not aware you do

I just ask that you forgive me too

For everything that was done was out of

Fear of losing you.

-Note to the surgeon

Reality:

Whether it is said out of fear of love on your

part

Fear of commitment

Fear that I don't understand love

And therefore cannot be in love

I have to take what you stated at face value

So I will no longer read between lines.

-Note to self

Unsaid:

Since we met

I had my reservations about your ability

To feel something for me

Me who was so broken

Unwed mother

Divorced mother of one

Lovely little girl whom you never got to meet

Surely if you did, you'd fall in love as I have

Because she is an extension of me and I

Am capable of being loved

Feeling loved

She would inherit love

Your love

As a father could love a daughter

I was so afraid of losing you

Afraid I was not good enough for you

Afraid you would leave after some time

Afraid of you not wanting the whole situation

Afraid of being honest

Afraid to lie

Afraid to show the real me

Afraid you deserved more

That you would realize that

And you would leave

As you did.

-Note to the surgeon.

Longing for your way

To say

You're sorry

-Apology never received

Unsaid:

I want to feel indifferent towards these
words.

I want to feel as though they were never said.

As if I hadn't read them

That you should take them back

As if *you* should not mean them.

-Note to the surgeon

Unsaid:

No one knows the pain and emotion

That comes with bearing your soul

Better than you have taught me

I love you

I do now

And will always

Love you

My heart has become accustomed

To the blows you throw

The deep wounds that cause shallow aches

That rocks me to sleep but not too deeply

For I am reminded of the pain through a

dream.

-Note to the surgeon

Unsaid:
Just because I am crazy in love with you

Doesn't make me crazy

Learn the difference.

-Note to the surgeon

Sent:

I am not perfect

You are not perfect

Let's combine our imperfections

And make our own version of perfect.

-Note to the surgeon

Read:

No response.

Unsaid:

I have never been in a fight

But I can imagine what it would feel like

 To have the wind knocked out of me

And being unable to breath

Fighting to get back to my feet

Trying to breathe deeply

While I crumble to my defeat

This is what your words have done to me.

-Note to surgeon

Unsaid:
You walked out the OR and told me

I needed a love transplant

That my love was shattered beyond repair

And just could not make it any longer

You rejected my love so coldly as you would

tell a family their loved one did not make it

and that you did your best

But they just simply could not get through it

You undemonstratively said you don't feel the

same unfortunately for me but fortunately for

you.

Leaving me to deal with the broken pieces of

unrepaired love.

-Note to surgeon

I kept seeing you as extraordinary

To the point where I began to feel ordinary.

-Note to the surgeon

Pain, joy, or sorrow

I write

I experience love and laughter

I write

I am happy, sad, hopeful, and glad

I write

So it's only right that during this

Moment of agonizing pain

That I write as I have written before

For the purpose of freeing myself and

My soul from the woes of love lost.

-Escaping

Shards of glass

Empty meaningless Expression

Of deeper emotions

That I cannot fathom

Could never get to the bottom

Of Them

For they overpower me

Overly aggressive

Not so much repressive

Emotions

They

Cling to me

Like a newborn baby clings to its binky

Like a mother to her daughter

Like a slave to freedom

Because I seldom

Know how to shake it

It overtakes its toll on me

Emotionally these

Unwelcomed emotions

Intrusive in nature

Don't know whether

To voice them out loud

Or to remain silent

And suffer

Because I cannot muster

Enough strength to overcome and sum up

These emotions

In a few lines of rhymes.

-Emotional

The revolution is NOT

Between my thighs

So keep your eyes

That are disguised

Wrapped in true lies

With lines I find

Can blind

My ability to unwind

The intertwined nature of such looks

For my heart is kind

But in time can grow cold

If I continue

To allow you

To stare

Into my bare soul.

-Wandering eyes

Funny thing about broken glass is

Even when you think you have swept it all up

There are pieces of shards of glass in the

cracks and hidden places that love to sneak

and poke your feet

They stop you in your tracks only to remind

you that time means nothing to the hidden

dangers of broken glass.

I guess it's what you do

When you realize that someone new

Has fallen in love with you

You mask your feelings and

Make sure you tell them

That you don't feel the same

And they're to blame

For falling

You stop calling

You run and hide

Because you can't decide

To commit to just one

And when you're done

Another one is lined up

The last one you're leaving stuck

On you

She's not sure what to do

But you are cool

Already seeing

Someone new

Your next victim

No one ever wins

This game you play

Not there to stay

And in the end you always

Have your way.

Not sure who told you it was okay to come and disturb my delicate peace. Though not completely solid, still broken at least I had a bit of feeling left in the peace I yearned for daily and eventually began to find. You took me from negative to positive in an instant I was excited, happy, overwhelmed with a feeling that something good had finally happened. You said you wanted to get to know me better in order to see whether we can be something eventually.

However, I did not know that this grace period meant that I could not be the real me, the version of me with broken pieces and shards of glass protruding from different angles; the version that can cut you without meaning to.

The mean version of me that creeps up when you least expect even when you thought all of the broken pieces were gone. They remained in the shadows and though no one knows when or even why they would hurt you without wanting to. All I can say I am sorry, I tried to hide these broken pieces but I guess they eventually got the best of me.

Know your place woman!!!

I guess I have never KNOWN my place

For if I did I would have remained broken

Dejected, dismayed, on the ground

Where you have thrown me

I don't know my place and I am not sure I ever

want to

-Rogue

Permission to Love

I am asking if it's okay to love you

As I have loved you all this time

Without permission or condition

I now want you to be consciously aware of

this love

In order that it might be reciprocated

In a way that is pleasing to me

Because I assure you my ways

Will always be pleasing to you.

-Permission granted

When you learn to speak your mind

And disagree with that which does not please

you

They say you have an attitude

You become part of the many reasons they

cannot deal

With a strong woman

Because you just do not know when

To be seen and not heard

You don't know when to

Curve your tongue

And NOT tell the man

When he is wrong

See this is why men stray from us, they say

Because with us and our mouths he could

never stay

He doesn't appreciate the strength

In a sense that says a lot about his confidence

A strong man can handle a strong woman any day

But a weak man...

Well, you know the rest.

I've come to the realization that I do not have to ignore or erase who I was with you because she is part of me too. What I can longer do is act as if she is the only part of me that I can recall. She is part of the story but not the entirety of the story. She has her place in each chapter but the story can be told without her. I can take what I loved about that girl I once was and incorporate her into the woman I have become. The painful moments she experienced brought strength to this new woman and I could not be who I am now had it not been for this seemingly fragile girl who withstood abuse and overcame in order for this woman to stand tall and strong. She is not abused she is strength.

I hurt too

I notice your absence too

I long for your voice too

I too need attention and affection

I no longer receive from you

Hold the applause

For you do not know me at all

You only see what I might be

On the surface

I cannot even face

Many monsters I've made

Through all of this

Hold your compliments

To me, they don't make sense

There is a girl in here somewhere

Who use to be considered beautiful

Standing in front of you

But she no longer sees in herself

What you see

And if she's your idea of beauty

Then she must be beautiful

That is if you say so

Hold your applause;

There is a dark side to me that you do not

know

So I must go before it begins to show

-Allusions

You walk around wanting to taste

Like a kid in a candy store

You are unaware of the damage

You cause to the many bites you've taken,

Not sure how or when you felt it was okay to

treat me like the rest of the candy you spit out

of your mouth after realizing it was far much

sweeter than you expected.

Picking up
the pieces

Please excuse me I forgot who I was

Who I was created to be

Who I have become through circumstances

Second and third chances

Given out of pity

Despite signs

showing me otherwise

Please excuse me,

I forgot who I was

I neglected the fundamental basis of my

existence

That it is you who finds a good thing

However, in pursuit of you

I lost me

And have become the watered down

washed out

Version of which you portrayed me to be

My apologies

Please excuse me I forgot who I was

-Amnesia

I normally would run when you call

And my flower would open up for you

Awaiting pollination

The anthers of your love would penetrate

The delicacy of my inner parts

That you and only you have access to

Because you solely have my heart

Chest to chest

Tongue to lips hands to hips

Don't get too caught up or aroused by this

For this is the last time

You will ever experience the thrust of

human connection

Upon further reflection

I've come to the realization

You no longer deserve

The softness and scent of my petals.

-Scented rose

Thank you for the lesson

I say thank you because I learned so much

from you

I learned that people who are vague

Are actually speaking clearly

The fact that they don't have a

A defined goal with their intentions

Should tell you everything

When you ask about their motive

Their response is laced with

More uncertainty than the question

They riddle their thoughts without

outward expression

Of Feelings

You the bystander reap the repercussions

Of their repressed pain

Stay away from these emotionally

withdrawn

People and their precipitous ways

Of dealing with the opposite sex

For their idea of love is completely

In opposition to yours

Forgive them

And release them with love.

-Letting go

The only thing I ever feared was losing you

Therefore, I have become fearless

For my deepest fears are realized.

-*Fearless*

You taste so sweet upon my lips

As you steal a kiss

Eyes closed

The sweetness radiates down to my bones

My soul knows

This feeling all too well

For with each other is where our spirits

dwell.

-Spirit in action

I take my coffee black

Will never apologize for that

I can taste the boldness of it

As the first sip reaches my lips

Bitter, rich, flavor

that I savor

It relaxes me

Beyond belief

For there is no need

To change the nature of the coffee bean.

-Bittersweet

How do I move on from here?

When the thought of you

With someone new makes my heart sink

I cannot fathom nor want to think

Of you without me

It seems this simple problem could never

be solved

The rules of mathematics cannot compute

Such monstrosity.

-You + me

I feel okay today

For the first time in a long time

I have peace within the thought of

continuing without you

Although I don't want to

-Nostalgia

As surely as the sunrise

My tired eyes will shine

While my heart cries

For blue skies

Cold tears dried

All pride aside

A tinge of hope and happiness

At the thought of you being a distant

memory

-Sunrise

I loved you before I understood

What love was, never experienced it in this

way

It was a feeling before I could put it in

words

It was a healing for my heart and mind

It was light, lovely, bold, pure,

Funny, mesmerizing, captivating,

Colorful, delicious, seductive,

Heartwarming, heartfelt,

Kind, loving, heart pounding,

Worthwhile, thoughtful, love.

-Love

Pick up the broken pieces

Put them back together

And begin to form the beautiful puzzle

That is you.

-Note to self

I am addicted to you

Like a crack addict

Back at it

Bad habit

I need to go cold off of you

-Addiction

Dear Anonymous

How could I have been so senseless?

To see you were never about my

happiness

You played with emotions

Being nothing more than infatuation

So don't indulge me with your so to speak

lies

Because in my eyes

You're nothing but a dog in disguise

Broke my heart

Tore me apart

Now dear Anonymous

Don't speak of a relationship in the past

Something that could never last

Tell me more I'm listening

Mesmerized by what you are missing

Now Dear Anonymous

How could you have been so cruel

Gave my heart to you

Played me for a fool

Thinking you loved me

Couldn't even see

What a four-legged creature you were

Yes you anonymous sir

You could run like water

But can't drop like rain

You don't seem to matter

Bringing nothing but pain

So Goodbye at Last anonymously

Never generously

It wasn't meant to be

Clearly, you were not man enough for me.

Beautiful am I

Beautiful are you

Profound beauty

And oh so true

True beauty is not shelf stored

Unhappy with yourself

And the pain you've endured

Criticized for I've been true

I feel you

Hear you

Your words hurt like a dagger

Plunging into my soul '

How could you know

Words I never said

Lines you never read

Beautiful am I

Beautiful are you

Can you imagine a world without hatred?

A world without you

-Beautiful

I know I can have

Just about any man I want

But I want you

For the beauty found in me

Surpasses time and space.

-Feeling myself

Love is not a garment

That you can put on and off

When it suits you

Love is eternal and internal

It is part of everything that is you

It is part of every cell

Every DNA strand

Countless

Like grains of sand

Love is not a choice

It is a necessity for all humanity

-Necessary love

I love the idea of being in love

I want to be so in love with you it hurts

I want to say things in

French like *Je mais manqué*

Because it is you that can bring these

wishes to reality.

To love is the perfect idea

We can inherit from our creator

We have an innate need to love and be

loved.

-Inherited love

I am with you in thought

Every moment of every day

I am with you holding your hand

Assuring you it is all going to be okay

-Always here

They say if I truly love you

I should let you go

But they don't know

Its' because I love

It is difficult for me to do so

I want to show the love in my actions daily

In order that you will really

Know that I love you for sure.

Someone else is capable

But no one is able

To love you the way that I do.

I am the one

I am the only one

Who sees you for who you truly are

I see the stars when we are where we are.

-Silly smirk

I want to love all things

Live through love

Show love

I want the light of love to shine through me

daily.

Letting go is the toughest part

I am afraid to let go

Afraid that if you come back

I will not be able to love you the same

That my heart will not overcome the

trauma

I will no longer be able to fall for you

And I guess I enjoyed the falling process

with you.

-*Falling out*

I grow cold with cheeks warm

At the thought of you with another

I cannot utter the words for the thought

Brings streams of tears that flood my

Emotions

Though inevitable

I'll eventually have to let go.

-Envy

Love me!!!
I need you to
Love me.

YOU truly are one of a kind
I just wish this one of a kind longed to be
mine.

The thought of you brings

Me to my knees literally

As they get weak

-Note to the surgeon

I gave you half of me

But you wanted ALL

You consumed me until

I barely had enough left

Not enough to survive

Let alone thrive

I realized that you are far too empty

No amount of me

Can fill you completely

-Emptiness

Wet, soft, warm

This love can do you no harm

-Note to the surgeon

Can I grow old with you?

Want nothing more

Than to grow with you.

-*Yearning*

Fell in love at first heartbeat first kick

The anticipation of arrival lasted 37 weeks

Induction was inevitable; finally, I was

able to fall deeper at first sight and every

day since. Half of me genetically but you'll

always have all of me, my heartbeat. You

are truly an angel that came to make life

much more meaningful.

-Baby girl

On the road to recovery

What can you do about broken glass?

Well, there isn't much you can do then to

ensure that you clean up daily even when

you cannot see the broken pieces any

longer. You know that you are cleaning up

for the purpose of getting rid of the pieces

you cannot see.

This ritual will become innate until all of

the broken pieces are gone.

Then you buy a new glass baby girl and are

more careful with the care of it for you are

well aware of the consequence of broken

glass.

One day you wake up feeling numb

After all the pain disappears

You feel indifferent towards anyone new

You become afraid that your heart is

incapable of love again.

-Fearful

I now fear not being able to replicate

The feelings I had for you

Someone new may enter my life

And I will do my best to feel something

But nothingness will remain

-Cold heart

I opened my eyes and began seeing
someone
But he isn't you
He doesn't make me laugh like you use to
I guess I should stop comparing him to you
Because you and he are two different
people
He is kind and sweet
Feels I am amazing
He sees the good in me
Because his peripheral isn't as active as
yours
He is able to focus
On me and what he feels matters
But he isn't you
I do not love him as I loved you
He doesn't make me feel like you use to

I don't get butterflies when I see him

I do not long to be with him like I use to

with you

I guess I am seeing him in an attempt to

substitute you

But he isn't you

Even though you did some messed up

things to my heart

Type of stuff that should have gotten

blocked for life

I guess we are both in need of optometry

So we can see each other for who we can

truly be.

-Eyes wide open

Tired eyes and lullabies

Kiss your tiny hand

And my heart cries

Pushing back the tears

Because in a few years

You'll be all grown up

And too cool to show love

Wanting to give you all I ever had

A warm home raised by mom and dad

That seems impossible

As I cannot get past your father

We cannot see eye to eye so I don't even
bother

Not to worry your pretty little heart

I'll never do anything to keep you two
apart

I will do my best with what I know now

And pray that God will continue to show me how

-Note to baby girl

-True love of my life

This isn't a revolving door I told him

You cannot come and go as you please

I won't allow it

My heart cannot take it

And my heart leaps in the background

Wanting to be wide open for him to enter

I'm sorry I told her, going with my mind on

this one

-Conflicted

Despite my stripes

I can hold my head up high

And say that I survived

-Survivor

I've learned to let people leave

Who are begging to be released

By their actions

-Unhinged

Unsaid:

The idea of fighting for a man

Has never crossed my mind

If it did I would dismiss it

And think of it as ghetto

A bit uncouth

The idea of physically fighting for you

That is if I had to

Is gladly welcomed

-Note to the surgeon

Nothing stands between you

And all the good you desire

But your own thoughts and feelings

-Unknown

-Unsaid:

I searched for understanding

And became further perplexed

I cannot fathom the depths of you

Bewildered by what you say

Versus what you do when we are together

The lack of feeling in your words

Leaving me to read between lines

But actions telling otherwise

Your eyes tell a different story

Than your lips

When you speak

Your kiss certainly confirms everything I

feel; yet you continually deny

Stating that THIS, US, WE are nothing more

than FUN.

-Note to the surgeon

Slowly feeling as if I am fading

Into your background

I stand in the shadows

As you rediscover

That which attracted you

To me in the first place

-Invisible

I am sure your heart

Speaks to mine

In a language

Only they can understand

She explained to me her fears

I told her to engulf herself in them

She told me she was hurting

I told to pursue that which is painful

She explained she was discouraged

I told her to find courage in the possibility

Of endless possibilities

She said she was fatigued

I told her to rest on her ability to be

What she visualizes herself being

She stated this brokenness has no

mending, I told her every broken soul

could be mended

She said she couldn't go further

I told her the choice to give up is not an

option, She begged for sleep

I told her to dream while she's awake

-Heart conversing with the mind. .

My lines define time

They come from the purest part of my soul

Realness is all you get with this.

-Deep

When you have someone looking up to you

You know that you have to go further than

You ever imagined

Regardless of what it looks like

You have to just keep moving towards

What seems to be impossible at the

moment

Know that it is possible

And you will connect the dots once you

arrive

Move blindly into your greatness

Allowing the power within to be your

guide.

-*Let love lead you*

-Unsaid

I am capable of loving

Myself, as much as I love you

I told you I loved you

You stated it is infatuation not love

As if you are incapable of being loved

-Note the surgeon

"STAY here tonight," I told him

"I have to be up early," he replied

"Let's get in the shower," I responded

"You go first and I 'll join," he said

"Hold my hand as we lay here"

 I responded

"Thought you were taking a shower," he

said "In a few minutes," I responded

"I just want to hear your heart beat a few

more times

 As I lie on your chest," I added

"Let's go take a shower," he said

Question for him!!

Who taught you to be emotionless?

-Note to the surgeon

Once you've experienced loved and loss

You fear the possibility of losing love

Therefore missing out on

The great feeling

Of falling in love

-Fearful

"Fall back!" My girlfriend says

"He isn't ready"

"Leave him be"

"His fickle ass ain't going nowhere"

Says my super educated M2-med student

Best buddy.

If only she knew that I tried

I am actively trying to yank my heart from

his grips

But I can't, she resides with him

Even though he only keeps her in the

foyer, she'd rather be there than nowhere,

for she cannot bear

The thought of not being in his presence.

The joys of finding, falling and losing love

I pray you only experience the first two

"Date!! Go on a few dates"

Find yourself....

I have not gone anywhere

That is in need of searching

I am here

Therefore I do not need to find me

I have always been here

Here is where I remain

No need to find anything

I am here

I am forever going to remain here

No need to find

That which isn't lost

I am here feeling, loving, losing,

Crying, falling, begging, rising

Winning, yearning

To be loved by the one man I love

STOP telling me to find *me*

I have never lost me

I lost love

There is a difference

-Losing

I am what you perceived me to be

The first time

No other perception matters

Before I bared the scars

Before you knew too much

Before you knew my secrets

Before you saw the marks

Of relenting courage to get through

Before all, you know and knew

I am what you perceived me to be

Perfect in that very moment

And every moment thereafter.

-First impression

Be kind,

Be kind to my heart

For she has no record of wrongdoing

That is not her duty

To keep track of all the wrong

That is for my mind to do

She only knows love

And forgiveness

She is always willing to forgive you

Ready to give one more chance

After the many chances, you've had with
her

Please be kind

Although she is gullible

To think it will be different this time

Be kind to my heart for she doesn't know
better.

-*Shattered heart*

I know it is difficult for you to digest

That I know for sure

You are the one

This comes from your own insecurity

And incapability to be loved

Has absolutely nothing to do with me

And who I perceive you to be

In my eyes, you are my best version of

perfect.

-Pure perfection

In an attempt to erase you

From my memory

I moved on physically

Last night, I tried to recreate reality

By moving on physically

Then I became empty

After which I cried

Wishing my soul would be untied

In that moment

An attempt to excrete

These feelings buried deeply

Within me

Every single cell in my body longs for you

You consume me

Even when I cannot see

My heart continues to seek

That which is nowhere near.

-Emotional

The stomping ground of love

Is where I want to remain

Forever in your arms

Want to be bound

By the sweetness of the love you bring.

-Warm embrace

Love me slowly

Love me gently

Love me lightly

Love me hard

Love me relentlessly

Love me rigidly

Love me rough

Love me with lust in your eyes

Love me in every way

Every single day

You have my permission to love me

differently.

-Feel the love

Cold is your heart

As it searches for warmth

Close to mine.

-Cold heart

Searching for you

While I am awake

In my dreams I find you

I find you and often do not want to let go.

-Daydreams

Some days I feel as though

We actually have a chance

Then you go on to show

The possibility of a chance

Is a quick glance at what could be

Perhaps will never be.

-Letting go

My heart is tired

Fatigued by the back and forth motion

She never stopped feeling

That is the reason it is difficult for her to

let go

Because she doesn't know how to just

STOP!!!!!!!!!!!!!

Feeling everything.

Table for one

As I sit in First Watch waiting for breakfast

alone

I am trying to picture you on the other side

Telling another silly joke

That I have heard a million times

But laugh like it's the very first time

When I hear the punch line

I listen with intention only because it's you.

-Note to the surgeon

I stand strong

I stand tall

I stand with all of the broken pieces

Glued together

But they're all holding me up somehow

I stand knowing that I will be okay.

-Finding strength

Some days you have to become a ferocious
lioness
They say the lion is the king of the jungle
But most days I am the queen

Fuck the king!!!!

The lioness is the **queen** of the jungle

I bring with me the fierceness of all she is
and will ever be.

Success comes from a good place

A place that does not know failure

A place that believes all things will work

out

A place that knows no boundaries

I am forever in that good place

Therefore;

I am all that my creator is

I am limitless.

-Life without limits

Who told you it was okay to walk around feeling like the victim?? Feeling as though the world owes you something
Look around you!! Everyone is striving to achieve his or her own goals. Achieve yours, stop comparing yourself to others you are not them and they aren't you. Do what is necessary for yourself and the one you gave birth to. She needs to see you stand not fall unfold not crumble.

I have bared it all; in an attempt that you would see that I am truly here for the long haul. I am real; I am in this with you. I bared it all that you would understand there is no ulterior motive that I don't have a sinister plan to take over your life. A hostile take over of your heart is all I am after, I want you to see me in the same way I see you. I am in need of you as I am in need of hydration. Don't think much about it until your life depends on submerging every cell in your body into what your body mostly consists of. I bare it all and will continue to bare everything so long as you will let me.

We are at the finish line

Thank you for going on this adventure

with me

I showed you my pain and you read

without judgment

Thank you for allowing me to reveal the

shards of glass that filled my heart and

mind for so long

I have placed them in these lines in order

to remove them from my soul

I can no longer hold on to them without

everything I endeavor to be shredded from

their jagged edges

I placed them on blank pieces of paper for

you to read

While not allowing them to pierce through

the pages and onto your life

133

Read them with caution for they have a way of trying to escape in order to become yours, they were once mine

Learn from them

Let them reside here on these pages never to cut through anyone again

All the pain, anger, anguish, love, laughter is here for you to enjoy at your leisure. It is written therefore it is done.

Thank you.

ABOUT THE AUTHOR

N. Akin is an American author and poet. She has been writing since she has had the ability to speak and write in English. N. Akin is also a pre-medical student in Florida and writes as a means of expressing her creativity. Ms. Akin has written other works that are not yet published pertaining to the empowerment of women. N. Akin believes poetry is the soul expressing itself through this art form.

www.ingramcontent.com/pod-product-compliance
Lightning Source LLC
Chambersburg PA
CBHW070555220526
45467CB00003B/1215